FROM ZERO TO ADULTHOOD

FROM ZERO TO ADULTHOOD

A 31-DAY PARENTING DEVOTION

RICK THOMAS

FROM ZERO TO ADULTHOOD:
A 31-Day Parenting Devotion

ISBN 978-1-966741-11-4

Rick Thomas

Edited by Sheron Wallace

Life Over Coffee
8595 Pelham Rd Ste 400 #406,
Greenville, SC 29615
LifeOverCoffee.com

Deuteronomy 6:4-9
Hear, O Israel: The LORD our God, the LORD is one.
You shall love the LORD your God with all your heart
and with all your soul and with all your might. And
these words that I command you today shall be on your
heart. You shall teach them diligently to your children,
and shall talk of them when you sit in your house, and
when you walk by the way, and when you lie down, and
when you rise. You shall bind them as a sign on your
hand, and they shall be as frontlets between your eyes.
You shall write them on the doorposts of your house
and on your gates.

For additional resources, visit
lifeovercoffee.com

Table of Contents

Scriptures

- Day 1: (Deuteronomy 6:6-7) From Zero To Adulthood
- Day 2: (1 Corinthians 11:1) Good Marriages
- Day 3: (Ephesians 4:32) Non-negotiable First Step
- Day 4: (Matthew 22:37-39) Two Rules for Children
- Day 5: (John 8:12) Orientation of the Home
- Day 6: (Luke 15:17-20) Before You Help Your Child
- Day 7: (Ephesians 4:29) Words Shape Children
- Day 8: (Galatians 5:22-23) Dads, a Child's First Picture
- Day 9: (Luke 6:45) Fewer Rules, More Attitude
- Day 10: (Proverbs 12:18) Fussy Parents, Insecure Kids
- Day 11: (James 1:20) Easy Way to Disqualify Yourself
- Day 12: (1 Thessalonians 5:14) Rule-Based Parenting
- Day 13: (Hebrews 12:6) On Critiquing Children
- Day 14: (Ephesians 2:8-9) Love Your Children Just 'Cause
- Day 15: (Proverbs 3:11-12) Discipline Comes from Love

Introduction

Parenting From Zero To Adulthood, 31-Day Devotional will teach you how to be a Bible-centered, God-centered parent. This biblically based devotional transcends cultures and applies to families who want to honor God by practicalizing His gospel into their family dynamic. The home is a laboratory where parents have the opportunity to provide a context and guidance for their children to mature into Christlike character qualities. The overarching goal of the parent is to release their children into the world as adults who humbly live under the authority of God.

The process of releasing them is incremental and appropriate to the individual child, as the parent cooperates with the unique narrative that God is writing into the child's life. Parents not only have the privilege to teach their children but also give them the most influential example of what they want them to be as they model the practical life of Christ before them. Parenting From Zero To Adulthood is full of tips, ideas, practices, and goals for you to implement immediately into your family. Don't worry about applying all of them; there are too many. Your best course of action is to prioritize the ones that most fit within your family and return to the others later. This devotional is an evergreen resource that never loses its value.

It may be more beneficial for you to select one devotion and integrate it into your family dynamic until it becomes a habit. Then, you can choose another chapter to implement. This is a 31-day devotional, but the journey of mastering this material extends beyond 31 days. My prayer is that the Spirit of God will enlighten your practical understanding and empower you to apply these truths in ways that transform you and your children for the glory of God.

Rick

Day 1

From Zero To Adulthood

And these words that I command you today shall be on your heart. You shall teach them diligently to your children, and shall talk of them when you sit in your house, and when you walk by the way, and when you lie down, and when you rise.

(Deuteronomy 6:6-7)

The parenting goal is to release your child into adulthood as an individual living under God's authority for His glory. This parenting process happens in three stages: Dependent Stage—0 to 2, Interdependent Stage—2 to 22, and Independent Stage—22+.

Each stage is a window of time that flexes depending on the child, parents, and situations. The stage is the context for the child to mature, revealing to the parents how to respond to each child uniquely. For example, some children will be independent long before their twenty-second birthday, while others will live with their parents long after their twenty-second birthday. The stages are suggestive, not binary.

Dependent Stage

From birth to the two-year mark, a child is dependent on their parents (or guardians). An infant can do little as far as taking care of himself. Even as early mobility begins, he does not have the mental or physical capacity to care for himself. By the time he is two years old, his ability to explore the world around him surpasses his psychological and physical capabilities. The combination of limited intelligence and ever-increasing independence converges to create a life stage that provides parents with incredible opportunities to lead their children. This stage is the time to lay the groundwork for heart characteristics that will shape his heart for the rest of his life. A few of those core traits are humility, honor, integrity, submission, obedience, honesty, discretion, love, serving, and self-control. A two-year-old's boundless energy and learning capacity provide the proactive parent with a pliable student for understanding what it means to be Christlike.

Interdependent Stage

As the child migrates from the dependent stage, the parent works at redrawing the lines by expanding the responsibilities for what the child should be doing and what the parent should be doing. This redrawing-expansion process continues throughout the child's life. The objective is always to move responsibilities away from the parents and to the child. Like a time-released capsule, the parent incrementally releases the child into God's world to live under His authority.

You will do nearly all the parental heavy lifting before the child is 12 years old. The teenage years are more about affirming or adjusting the prior parental work from the previous decade. Like slow-setting cement, his manner of living (Ephesians 4:22) is in place as he experiences an inward and increasing compulsion to do life independently.

The parent's primary work in the child's heart is the first half of the interdependent stage (2 to 12). The last half of this time (12 to 22) is when the parent motivates the child to continue as he is or refine his inadequacies. Most of the time, it's a combination of the two. The child is mostly okay, and the parent leads him to maturity (Hebrews 10:24-25). Or the child is mostly bad, and the parent is looking for reinforcements through intervention, hoping the child does not bankrupt his life.

Independent Stage

This final stage is releasing your child into God's world as an individual under His authority. There is no perfect release age; each child and situation are different. The independent years do not mean parents stop parenting, but their roles in the child's life dramatically change.

Time to Parent

1. What stage best represents your child?
2. How are you maturing your child through that stage?
3. What is one goal that will help him be more mature within his current stage?
4. What is your plan to implement this aim?

Day 2

Good Marriages

Be imitators of me, as I am of Christ.
(1 Corinthians 11:1)

The Bible is not a parenting book, so it gives so little parenting advice. It is a relationship book. Rather than providing you with parenting tips, it provides you with a plethora of information about how to have great relationships within any community construct, whether it's marriages, families, churches, businesses, friends, or neighbors.

If you want your child to learn how to live in and enjoy wonderful relationships, your primary goal must be to show them the One who perfected relational living: He is Christ. You want them to be Christlike. Every Christian parent wants their child to be an authentic and maturing representation of Jesus, which leads to an important question: What is the most effective way to teach your child how to be like Jesus? You export your life to them. You must become a living, breathing, walking example of what you want your children to become.

Parents should not be parenting as much as they should export their marriage relationship to their children. Truthfully, parents are exporting their marriage relationship to their children, whether the parents know it or not, because there is no other option. The real question is, what is your marriage teaching your child about relationships?

Children spend nearly twenty years soaking in their

parents' lives while making determinations as to whether they want to emulate what they are absorbing. Living in a relationship is why the most effective parenting is not how to parent better but how to relate well to your spouse. Every spouse can display how to live with another sinner before their children effectively, and no sinner is closer to you than your spouse. The powerful impact of a stable marriage becomes your most effective training tool. Your children will observe you doing the very thing you want them to do as they create their future community relationships.

Your marriage is a visual expression of what it means to love God and someone else supremely (Matthew 22:36-40). If you have not been a good model of what it means to relate well with another person, specifically, you have not lived biblically well with your spouse, today is the day for you to change. Ideally, both spouses should repent mutually, but that is rarely the case. Usually, one spouse becomes more aware of the adverse effects of their marriage on the children long before the other spouse. If you're the only one willing to live an authentic Christian life before your children, I appeal to you to do it.

You must actively, daily, and practically live out what you want everyone in your home to be, including your wayward spouse. Give your child a good picture that will be different from any poor images in your home. Ask the Father to give you the grace and boldness to give your children that portrait. In a perfect world, both parents realize their imperfect exportation of Christ to their children. They see how it led to a confused and frustrating picture for their kids to emulate. This kind of parental failure motivates humble and broken parents to fix the marriage, but, as you know, we do not live in a perfect world.

Time To Parent

1. What have you taught your children about how to relate well with another sinner—specifically your spouse?
2. If you have not done a decent job emulating Christ to your children, what will you do to change today?

Day 3

Non-negotiable First Step

Be kind to one another, tenderhearted, forgiving one another, as God in Christ forgave you.

(Ephesians 4:32)

Christians enjoy and benefit from the gospel because of forgiveness (see Romans 10:9, 13). For example, we confessed our sins and requested forgiveness, and our kind Lord forgave us. Confession, forgiveness, and reconciliation are the stepping stones to happiness (Deuteronomy 33:29). If you want a happy home, you must imitate God at this crucial point (Ephesians 5:1).

During the first five years of our marriage, I never asked Lucia to forgive me for any sins I committed against her. That is a staggering thing to say. Let me state the obvious here: my view of God, humanity, and sin was sub-biblical. My gospel understanding and practices suffered because of my weak theological perspectives (Hebrews 5:12-14; 1 Peter 2:2-3). One of the most transformative relationship-building questions you will ever ask another person is, "Will you forgive me?" Forgiveness is how your relationship with God began, and the process is similar for His image-bearers (Genesis 1:27; Ephesians 5:1).

A Christian who does not regularly ask for forgiveness is like the son of a millionaire who has no awareness of his daddy's fortune. Or even worse, he is aware of his father's wealth but refuses to benefit from it (1 Peter 1:4). Forgiveness is a free and unlimited gift from the Lord. Still, it requires humility to access it, whether you are asking for it from someone or granting it to someone. The person who is not regularly asking for forgiveness is either self-deceived, is a pretender, or is living in denial of the doctrine of sin. A forgiven person—who is authentically residing in the grace of God's forgiveness—is willing to ask for and grant forgiveness. Reflect on these seven steps to see where you are in building a happy home.

Seven Simple Steps

1. **BE HONEST:** You know when you sin (1 John 1:7-10; Romans 2:14-15).
2. **WALK IN THE SPIRIT:** When you sense God's illumination, step into it. Don't run, but obey Him in all things.
3. **PRACTICE FORGIVENESS:** Don't say "I'm sorry" or apologize. Push the biblical envelope by pursuing radical reconciliation. Ask for transactional forgiveness.
4. **START WITH GOD:** Don't ask others to forgive you while not asking God to forgive you. All sin is a sin against God.
5. **BE SPECIFIC:** "Will you forgive me for (name the sin)?" Let them know that you know how you have sinned. Do not let them let you off the hook. Make them forgive you. Be convincing, persuasive, and unrelenting in your pursuit of forgiveness.
6. **SURRENDER:** Give up your rights by submitting yourself to the authority of God and His Word. Choose no other option until you are released from your sins and restored to those you offended.

7. **REMEMBER:** There is power in forgiveness. After the Father had executed His Son on the cross (Isaiah 53:10), He made it possible to release any person from the guilt and punishment that all sin deserves (Romans 6:23). As a Christian, you have the grace-empowered privilege to live daily in a guilt-free home if you are honest with yourself, God, and others.

After Lucia and I began to see the gospel with more practical clarity, we started to live in a sanctification sweet spot that radically changed our home. We replaced the guilt, burden, shame, unresolved conflict, and the proverbial pink elephants flying around the room with the love, joy, peace, hope, and mercy that Christ offers through practicing forgiveness.

Time To Parent

1. Would you characterize your home as a place where confession and forgiveness regularly happen? If not, why not?
2. Are all the members of your home committed to practical transactional forgiveness? Please explain.
3. What specific plan will you implement to help motivate all your family members to be forgiveness askers and receivers?

Day 4

Two Rules for Children

You shall love the Lord your God with all your heart and with all your soul and with all your mind. This is the great and first commandment. And a second is like it: You shall love your neighbor as yourself.
(Matthew 22:37-39)

Biblical parenting incrementally releases children from your rules and authority while placing them under the most influential governing dynamic known to humanity—to love God and others supremely. If your child's heart is motivated and governed by those two truths, and you help him to embrace that kind of affection for God and neighbor, you will serve your child well.

Your parenting objective is to lead your child to Christ so he can learn to love God and others as he loves himself. No other code of conduct or religious system could provide anything better. Living under God's authority with a satiable love for Him is God-glorifying, soul-satisfying, and neighbor-affecting. The most remarkable thing about the two great commandments is that there are only two of them. Too many rules make one's head swim. The rule-based life is a yoke of slavery that whittles you down to an awkward, out-of-step conservatism, or it exasperates you to the point of throwing the rules out the window and walking away from God.

Suppose you want to teach your child rules and show him how to love God and his neighbor as he loves himself. Let the Lord's primary rules be your top two. Always remember that these rules have more to do with your child's attitude than his behaviors. You cannot love God and others as you love yourself unless the Lord has transformed your inner being. This need makes shepherding a child's heart important because all behaviors—good or bad—flow from his attitude. Isn't that true for you? Your attitude about God determines how you respond to Him. And your attitude about (your neighbor) determines how you react to (your neighbor).

Because loving God and others is the end game, you must carefully consider how you motivate your child toward that God-glorifying goal. You have to determine if what you are doing as a parent is helping to facilitate that kind of change. If it is not, you must discard it. The first step in this transformative process is for your child to be born again (John 3:7), which you cannot make happen. Only the Lord can grant spiritual transformation to anyone (2 Timothy 2:24-25; 1 Corinthians 3:6). Your job is to point your child to the gospel while pleading with God to implement this essential first step. The two ways you can cooperate with the Lord in this process are—in this order—model the gospel before your child and teach him about the gospel. Teaching the gospel is more evident to most Christians than modeling the gospel, which is why I've listed four ways you can model the gospel to your child, with the hope the Lord will regenerate him so he can experience the empowerment to love God and others supremely.

Time to Parent

1. **MODEL GRATITUDE:** If your child were free to speak the truth to you, would he say gratitude is what characterizes you? (1 Thessalonians 5:18)

2. **MODEL KINDNESS:** What does your child experience more from you: your kindness to him or your disappointment in him? (Romans 2:4)

3. **MODEL SERVING:** Do you serve in such a way that your kid is motivated to emulate your servant's heart? (Mark 10:45)

4. **MODEL REPENTANCE:** Are you an active repenter, and is your child a regular recipient of your requests for forgiveness? (1 John 1:7-10)

Practicing these four Christ characteristics will motivate your child to love God and others more than himself.

Day 5

Orientation of the Home

Jesus spoke to them, saying, "I am the light of the world. Whoever follows me will not walk in darkness, but will have the light of life."

(John 8:12)

J esus was clear when He said you must follow Him if you want to walk in the light. The opposite is also true: if you do not follow Him, the only option is darkness, as you follow someone or something else. Every relational construct has followers and leaders, which begs the question, who is the leader of your home?

After a lot of living and a good bit of failing, I have learned that my family cannot trust me to be the spiritual leader of our home. This truth is no secret to any of us. I had proven my inability to lead well and had put my sin on display in our home too many times. I needed to acknowledge what my family already knew about me and why someone else must be in charge of our home. They needed to know that someone more capable than me would spiritually lead us. Anything that replaces Christ as the leader of your home is idolatry. God replacements suck the spiritual life out of what should be a vibrant God-centered home. The first step in orienting your home to God is to speak about what needs to change. You will not be able to do this without the humbling power of the gospel working in the hearts of the parents and children. The two most common problems in the disoriented home are child-centered families and the passive husband.

- **CHILD-CENTERED:** Some families make their children the centerpiece of the home. Everything revolves around them. The typical mom in a child-centered home can spend ten to fifteen years in a minivan serving the activity-centered child. These kids can become increasingly self-centered as life revolves around their social and activity preferences. Many of these children rarely learn humility, respect, or submission. They typically do not love God or others as much as they love themselves because their parents have not prioritized those two truths.
- **PASSIVE HUSBAND:** The spiritually passive man is another common problem in a disoriented family. The stagnant male leader in the home is where the wife takes more of the spiritual leadership role, while the man is preoccupied with other things that align with his self-centered preferences. Perhaps he has no template for what a male leader should be or no values for what male leadership should be. Regardless, the passive husband's home is an upside-down family.

If your home's orientation centers on the wrong person or incorrect things, please understand that there is no way to correct the problems unless the husband and wife are willing to talk about the disorientation and make a practical plan to reorient their family so Christ is leading it. If it is impossible to talk about these things—for whatever reason—I appeal to you to find someone who can walk you through the problems. The disoriented home rarely auto-corrects; if it continues, the inevitable fallout will break your heart.

Time to Parent

Who would you say is the point person in your home? Who is spiritually leading your family? If the Lord is not the leader, consider why it is not happening. Here are a few things to reflect upon:

1. Do you know what it looks like for Christ to lead the family? Please discuss this.
2. Is the husband regularly encouraged to lead the family? If not, why not?
3. Is the wife willing to submit to her husband's leadership? If not, why not?
4. Do you have a child-centered home and don't know how to change it? Please explain.
5. Will you begin the process of talking about how everyone can submit to Christ as the spiritual leader of your home? When will you start, and what is your plan?

Day 6

Before You Help Your Child

When he came to himself, he said, "How many of my father's hired servants have more than enough bread, but I perish here with hunger! I will arise and go to my father, and I will say to him, 'Father, I have sinned against heaven and before you. I am no longer worthy to be called your son. Treat me as one of your hired servants.'" And he arose and came to his father.

(Luke 15:17-20)

You can only help a child if he wants help. If your child is not serious about change, your care for him will have a limited impact. Your primary parental role is waiting on the Lord as He brings your child to an end of himself. You can motivate him all along the way as you cooperate with the story God is writing in your child's life, but you cannot change your child no matter how hard you try (2 Timothy 2:24-25).

The Prodigal Son narrative in Luke's Gospel gives you a template that will help govern your heart as you wait for your child to change. Notice the four sequential steps that led to the Prodigal's transformation.

#1: END—*He Came to an End of Himself*
The end of himself is always the beginning of change. The end is the necessary first step because a child will often experience worldly sorrow rather than godly sorrow (2 Corinthians 7:10). He feels caught between his sin and its horrible consequences, so he says he is ready to change. A few months later, he returns to his sin like a dog returning to its vomit (Proverbs 26:11).

#2: LIGHT—*He Sees The Light*
When your child gets to an authentic end of himself, he will experience God's empowering illumination. You won't have to tell a repentant person what to do. The repentant individual automatically knows how, when, and why to do the will of God. He's like a wind-up toy. God winds him up with divine favor, and your job is to get out of his way because his heart is motivated to transform. God will use your counsel, but your counsel will have little effect if the Lord is not actively illuminating the child.

#3: PLAN—*He Makes A Plan For Repentance*
After God turns the light on, the former rebel will be proactively thinking through a plan of repentance. Notice what the Prodigal did. Before he acted on his plan of repentance by going to his father, he sat in the hog lot and scripted a plan for repentance. Premeditated repentance is a crucial step. Isn't that your testimony? You came to an end of yourself, God illuminated your mind, you premeditated your change, and you began working your plan for repentance.

#4: ACT—*He Acts Out His Plan*
He put a wooden stake through the heart of his old self and jumped on the road to repentance. When you see a repentant person—like the Prodigal's daddy saw his son—God will have already changed him. There is nothing left

for you to do but forgive and love him. If your child needs to change but has not yet come to the end of himself, the first thing you should do is wait as you ask the Lord to bring your child to the beginning of change, which is the end of himself.

Time to Parent

1. How do you act like the Holy Spirit in your child's life? For example, do you become impatient with your child while trying to speed up the change process?
2. Talk to God and a close friend, asking both to help you learn practical patience as you cooperate with the Lord in transforming your child.

Day 7

Words Shape Children

Let no corrupting talk come out of your mouths,
but only such as is good for building up, as fits the
occasion, that it may give grace to those who hear.
(Ephesians 4:29)

I had a conversation with our son when he was younger, sharing with him how he would be my replacement. It was a sobering thought. One day, our son will grow up and become a practical demonstration of what I have modeled for him. The good and the bad of my life work together to bring shape to his adult life.

When I am older and my pace slows, he will jog onto the field of life, take the ball from me, and run into the next generation. He will likely assume the role of a husband and a father as I go to the sidelines to join that cloud of witnesses with the other aging athletes past their prime. I will become an observer of my work in his life. Your children are like moldable pieces of clay that God has given to you to shape by teaching them about God, guiding them to God, and releasing them into God's world.

The primary way you mold your child is by the life you live before him and the words you speak to him. Do not be self-deceived about this matter: you are the most impactful picture that your child will ever see. And believe me, he is closely watching you. Each day, your child examines, ponders, analyzes, and determines if your life is worthy of his emulation. Though he will probably never tell you these things, your life actions are inevitably causing positive and negative reactions that will set the trajectory of your child's life. While it is true that God can overwrite your works in your child's life, you are not allowed to presume on His grace (Psalm 19:13).

One of the most potent ways you influence your children is your opinion of them (Proverbs 29:25). How you think about your children is connected to their greatest joys and biggest disappointments. You can lift them with your words or devastate them with what you say to them. Your comments are like ready soldiers that march off your tongue to destroy or build up those around you. In that way, you are no different from your children: the opinion of your heavenly Father means everything to you.

Mercifully, He loves you to death (Isaiah 53:10; John 3:16). Because of His great love for you, your soul is set free to be the best child that you can be in His world. You want to model your heavenly Father's affection for you to your kids. You want them to hear and feel your words of encouragement (Romans 2:4). You have the power to build them up and have the authority to tear them down. All of that power sits on your tongue and comes from your heart (Luke 6:45).

Time to Parent

Because of the gospel, you benefit from God's boundless love. Now, He calls you to imitate Him to your children (Ephesians 5:1). These questions will help you examine how you're imitating your heavenly Father to your child.

1. The gospel informs you that God is pleased with you (Romans 8:31). Is your child more aware of your pleasure or displeasure in him?

2. The gospel speaks peace into your chaos and transforms you. How are you speaking into your child's life to bring God-glorifying transformation to him?

3. You act out the gospel by serving rather than expecting others to serve you (Mark 10:45). What concrete and practical ways are you helping your child?

Day 8

Dads, a Child's First Picture

But the fruit of the Spirit is love, joy, peace, patience, kindness, goodness, faithfulness, gentleness, self-control; against such things, there is no law.
(Galatians 5:22-23)

We were sitting at an intersection when our then 6-year-old daughter said, "Daddy, that Blues Clues paw print is orange." This instance was the second time it happened with our children. Blues Clues was a once-popular kid's program about a dog named Blue who would leave his paw print in different places during the show.

Each paw print sighting would reveal a clue. The viewers would solve the riddle once the TV host found all three of Blue's paw prints. Blue's paw print was, of course, blue. Our child knew of only blue pawprints, which is why she was baffled to find an orange one on the bumper of a car. The orange one represented Clemson University. She had no clue about Clemson University, so it confused her when she saw the orange paw print. Young children have only one reference point. In psychology, this is called mutual exclusivity.

Our child established her reference point by prior knowledge of a blue paw print that she had learned from a TV show. She also described the hair on my arms as fur rather than hair. Her previous experience with stuffed animals gave her that interpretation. Children cannot think outside their tight, immature box, which explains why our other child questioned me when I drove faster than fifty-five miles per hour. He remembered me saying the speed limit is fifty-five miles per hour. It did not dawn on him how there could be different speed limits or how it's practically impossible to drive exactly fifty-five miles per hour.

As our children matured, they learned how to parse things more broadly. They did not continue to think in restrictive, undeviating, black-and-white parameters. Our daughter discovered many types, colors, and sizes of paw prints. Her tight singularity about Blues Clues was not always her restrictive reference point. But back then, that is how she saw life, which is how all children interpret life. One size does fit all for younger children. Applying this concept to the word father should be a sober call for any dad.

A young child cannot think about alternate possibilities when interpreting what a father is supposed to be. They believe in their isolated experience with their unique fathers. They can't know what they can't know, and if the child does not know anything different, they must work with what they have. For example, I'm an older father, compared to the statistics. Most parents with children my age are under fifty years old. I'm not. It is humorous as our children have realized I'm older than their friends' parents.

From their perspective, all parents are over fifty. When they hear of other younger parents, they must recalibrate their thinking. Though they can readjust, some things require more recalibrating. One of those things is how they think about God the Father. I have counseled many adults still struggling with how they relate to God as a Father. This recalibration problem is almost always due to how they relate to their fathers. This father/child problem is significant and can be spiritually crippling. Though our former six-year-old did overcome the complexity and diversity of paw prints, it is much harder to overcome dads who provide a dysfunctional picture of what a father should be.

Time to Parent

1. An excellent template for what God is like is Galatians 5:22-23. Dad, will you take each of those nine elements and assess how well you imagine God the Father to your children?

Day 9

Fewer Rules, More Attitude

The good person out of the good treasure of his heart produces good, and the evil person out of his evil treasure produces evil, for out of the abundance of the heart, his mouth speaks.

(Luke 6:45)

A right heart attitude will create the right behaviors, but knowing and obeying all the rules does not mean the heart is good or even agrees with the actions. From the inside out is the Bible's way to parent children, not merely outward assessments. Though regulations will give you the desired behaviors you pray for when your kid is young, those rules cannot change your child's heart.

Your primary parenting target is always your child's heart if you have any hope of helping him live well in God's world. Though God initiates all change through the instrumentation of His grace, you must cooperate with the Lord in parenting your children. You can do this if you give your kids fewer rules and more attitudes. When your child is older, he will choose the behaviors that will be part of his life. Those practices will come from his heart—the person he is at the core of his being. So, while he is under your roof, you want to help him mature in the right heart attitudes, which will shape those behaviors. Four of those heart attitudes are affection, honor, gentleness, and gratitude. Let me illustrate them for you.

- Parent your child to have affection for Christ (Matthew 22:36-40).
- Parent your child to honor you and his siblings (Romans 12:10).
- Parent your child the value of a gentle spirit (Galatians 6:1-2).
- Parent your child to be a grateful person (1 Thessalonians 5:18).

Galatians 5:22-23 provides more heart attitudes to use in your parenting. The fundamental idea is that if your child is learning the rules that Christians obey but is not maturing from the heart in things like affection for Jesus, respect for others, gentleness within relationships, and spontaneous gratitude, you must rethink how you're parenting your child. A word of caution is that you want to ensure your training is not only dedicated to Bible instruction times. Though teaching is good, modeling is better. You can teach your child each morning at 7 AM—or whatever time best fits your schedule—but your most effective training is those pneumatic moments throughout your day as you keep in step with the Spirit of God, responding to what the Lord is writing into your life. Spontaneous life moments are the times that reveal the authentic heart.

Rules can be good because you can predetermine your responses, but life is not neat, controlled, and scripted. It would be best to be pneumatic because that is how life comes at you. You can be Spirit-led if the Spirit has previously shaped your heart. This kind of attitude is what you're looking for in yourself, and it is what you want to model before your child.

Time to Parent

1.   The first thing to do is examine your last disappointment, especially a relational one. How did you respond? What did your disappointment reveal about your heart? Are there any changes you need to make?

2.   Take notice of this step. If your heart is not trained and managed by God, you will not be an effective teacher to your child. You must identify any sinful heart attitudes and change them. As you do this, you will position yourself to teach your child proper biblical attitudes

Day 10

Fussy Parents, Insecure Kids

There is one whose rash words are like sword thrusts, but the tongue of the wise brings healing.
(Proverbs 12:18)

Mable couldn't get a handle on her insecurity. Burdened by a failed marriage, teenage children in rebellion, and too many relational conflicts to count, she was frustrated, angry, and bewildered at how the same old things kept happening to her. Though she recognized she had a lifelong problem with anxiety, fear, and insecurity, she did not understand it or why it had such a stranglehold on her life. As we began to chat, it quickly became apparent how her fear had initially gripped her life. Mable was the product of parents who had an ongoing, unresolved conflict. Mable had fussy parents!

Kids know they need their parents to protect them. Though they cannot articulate this desire, they can sense when things are not right in the home. When things become dysfunctional, they typically become afraid. I have heard many adult children talk about how their fussy parents left them feeling alone, vulnerable, and scared that something terrible was about to happen.

Because of our Adamic nature, fear comes with the human package. Children will panic when bad things happen, particularly between the only two people in their world who can protect them. Mable said she panicked on the inside but had no one to share her fearful thoughts with. She internalized them because her primary protectors were on the verge of a marital meltdown. She said there were many nights she would ball up and cry herself to sleep as she listened to the verbal sparring on the other side of her bedroom wall.

Her parents told her that no one in their church was ever to find out what was going on in the home. Mable kept her mouth shut, which only exacerbated the fear that was slowly sucking the life out of her. She lived with ever-present insecurity that one day, she would come home only to find her parents gone. Because she could not understand her chaotic home life, she drew the worst kinds of conclusions about the problems in her family. Mable said most of their arguing was about money. Though it seemed like all roads led to an argument, it was money that kept coming up again and again.

After a while, she stopped asking her mom for things. Mable never said how badly she wanted what all her friends had whenever there was a new fad or fashion. Her mom never picked up on the knot in Mable's heart that was twisting tighter and tighter. By the time Mable was a teen, she had begun to look for security through any means possible, though she did not dare to try out for anything like sports or cheerleading because her fear of failing was too intense.

Her avenue of escape was through boys, a path that was the total unraveling of her life. Her craving for protection and love was so intense that it blinded her to the common sense she should have possessed. She knew all her boyfriends were using her. Still, she dismissed the notion because of her fifteen years of pent-up cravings for security that uncontrollably lapped up any affection and approval she could find. She was easy picking, and she was glad. From her perspective, manipulating love from others was the path to freedom.

Time to Parent

1. Mable's story is fictional, but it's too true for many boys and girls. These young people are now adults, and the fallout still lingers in their souls and relationships. If you have a fussy home, you must repent right now. Do not delay. Find help today.

Day 11

Easy Way to Disqualify Yourself

The anger of man does not produce the righteousness of God.

(James 1:20)

Too often, parents with sinning children focus too quickly on the disruptive child as they overlook their reactions to their disappointing child. Here are two questions that will help you avoid this parenting problem: How would you describe your relationship with the Lord? How are you practically living that relationship out daily inside your home?

If you do not respond appropriately to these questions, you will likely be unable to meet your long-term parenting goal of cooperating with God in helping your child become more like Jesus. It would be like trying to make a car go forward without an engine under the hood. The parents are the engine that drives the family forward in pursuing practical God-centered living. If the parents are not right with God and each other, they will make it exponentially more difficult for their child to become Christlike. While many children can become practical Christ-lovers despite their parents, it would be presumptuous to expect them to do this without them participating in the process (Psalm 19:13-14). If you sin in response to your child's sin, you are, at that moment, disqualified from helping your child change. Let me give you a parabolic illustration: A boy falls to the ground. A man jumps on top of the boy while he is on the ground.

The boy who fell is more concerned about the man who jumped on top of him than the reason he fell. To sin is to fall, which is what the boy did. The parent then sinned in response to the child's sin. The one at the bottom of the pile will be more concerned about the one who jumped on him than his reason for falling. The fallen child cannot effectively do anything about his fall until his parents stop complicating the matter by jumping on him after he falls. In football, they call it piling on. That is when someone from the opposing team jumps on a previously tackled player. Piling on your fallen child will keep you from appropriately dealing with the areas in his life that need transformation, and you will make your child afraid of you. Each time a parent sins by anger in response to their child's sin, they will put the child on his heels. Anger from a parent complicates a child's heart.

Children crave love and protective care, but parents can disrupt these good aims if they do not bring their anger into submission to Christ (2 Corinthians 10:3-6). Fear-motivated children go into a defensive, tightening up, and shutdown mode as a matter of self-preservation. The parents may tempt the child to lie about what he did because he's scared of how his parents will react. In those moments of tension, he will sense that the wrong response could set a parent off. He will put up a wall as a means to protect himself, which will circumvent any possibility of a grace-filled conversation with him.

Time to Parent

1. Accurately describe what is going inside you when your child disappoints you (James 4:1-3).
2. As you understand what is going on inside your heart, you can isolate the idolatries that cause you to choose anger. Start walking out repentance, which will position you to help your child the next time he falls.
3. In addition to personal and practical repentance, find ways to encourage your child (Romans 2:4). Before, you were de-motivating him by sinful anger. Now, you can motivate him by identifying the evidence of God's grace in his life.

Day 12

Rule-Based Parenting

And we urge you, brothers, admonish the idle, encourage the fainthearted, help the weak, be patient with them all.

(1 Thessalonians 5:14)

Being authoritarian is a good thing because, as image-bearers, we want to emulate our Father. Thus, we must learn to live under God's authority and learn how to model it. However, if authoritarianism is our only parenting method, it may scuttle our children's individualized sanctification needs.

Exclusive authoritarianism creates a black-and-white world where adherence to the rules is the only way children can earn a parent's favor. This parenting model is like a big authoritarian umbrella. If the children stay under the umbrella, they will be fine—so the strict parent would want you to believe. "If you do what I say, you will be okay. But, if you go against my rules, you'll be in trouble." The problem is that a child's heart does not function this way. The authoritarian parent must give his children more than rules; he must nurture them.

Thus, exclusive authoritarianism is a lazy parenting model. The parent lays out the rules and demands everyone's allegiance. He legislates morality. If the family lives in an authoritarian culture, subjective evidence will support the strict parent's way of doing things, i.e., the younger children will obey. When children raised in these legalistic homes push those boundaries, there are nearly always dire consequences, which rarely include a restorative plan. Authoritarian homes are punitive homes. The authoritarian parent says, "See, I told you if you don't obey me, this is what happens."

The more timid children will salute Dad's flag and never buck his system because the consequences are not worth it. Conditional love wrapped in rules is an awful parenting model. It may keep the children separated from the world while young, but it will not equip them to engage the world when they step out from under their dad's authoritarian umbrella. God has called us to a pneumatic life; we are to walk in the Spirit as He guides us. The Spirit teaches us how to live moment by moment in His world.

The Lord did not give us a restrictive list of rules to follow. Instead, He gave us an organic relationship that factors in the uniqueness of each of His children. Any parent with more than one child knows this, which is why it's unwise to lay down a blanket list of rules and make the kids obey while motivating them by fear if they cross the line. That model does not rear children. Instead, it rears robots who do not have the practical equipping to live in the culture while engaging Christ. The only kind of person they could engage is someone like them, someone from their rule-based culture.

The authoritarian parent must also be a nurturing parent. He teaches them straightforward ways to live as he discerns each child and helps the child overcome his unique Adamic brokenness and other shaping influences. You see this idea in 1 Thessalonians 5:14, where Paul talks about three different kinds of people and gives the Thessalonians three distinct ways to care for them. He did not say that all three people groups obey the same strict code of conduct.

Yes, there are biblical ethics to live by, but the Bible is more than an ethics manual. Children are relational beings who need specific care. If we don't provide that kind of unique parenting, legalism is our only option, which will prove to be destructive.

Time to Parent

1. Is your parenting model legalistic? Please explain.
2. Is your parenting model a reaction to legalism, to where you parent with a sloppy kind of grace devoid of rules? Please explain.
3. Do you know how to provide both structure (rules) and support (nurture) so your child knows what God expects but is not bound to a black-and-white world of standards? Please explain.

Day 13

On Critiquing Children

For the Lord disciplines the one he loves, and chastises every son whom he receives.

(Hebrews 12:6)

If a person's parenting model primarily consists of bringing critique from a heart of personal frustration, the parent's model needs to change. Biblical parents center their primary communication with their children on love, not criticism. God's corrective care is always in the context of love. He disciplines the one He loves, and when you experience God's corrections, you're acutely aware that He loves you.

God is continuously surveying the scene of your life not to critique you but to pour out His extravagant love on you. A gospelized parent is similar, constantly surveying the scene of a child's life because he loves his child and wants to motivate him toward Jesus. The parent is not surveying the scene because he's looking for opportunities to criticize his child. Instead, he wants to catch his child getting it right. Perhaps your child does something wrong, and you must correct him. If so, the Bible's mandate on helping trapped people is with a spirit of gentleness (Galatians 6:1-2). But, of course, there are times when you can overlook the offense because you don't want to nickel and dime your child to death, and in many cases, the problem will pass.

You can determine these things by asking yourself if it is an episode or a pattern you observe in his life. If it's an episode, maybe you can let it go. If it's a developing pattern, you probably have to deal with it. You never want to withhold correction when it is needed because there are times when corrective care is the only way to help your child change. Still, when you do it, you want to imitate God in how you do it (Ephesians 5:1). Therefore, it would be best to contextualize your critique in the overwhelming, never-able-to-fully-express-love you have for your child.

Lucia and I like to think of it in a ten-to-one ratio: for every one negative thing we must say to our child, we have already identified, isolated, and encouraged him with ten good things that we have observed in his life. This ten-to-one ratio is a rule-of-thumb concept, not a legalistic one. It conveys the idea that love for your child is more significant than your disappointment. If you do not put money in the bank of your child's heart, you will bankrupt him. Furthermore, you will tempt him with all kinds of sins, like deceit, as he hides his actions because he knows that Captain Critique is just around the corner with a quick-to-speak and slow-to-listen mindset (James 1:19).

One of the most valuable parenting tips that served us when our children were younger was spending time during the day sneaking around our house trying to catch our children doing well. Though it's easy to catch them doing wrong, loving them enough to find evidence of God's grace in their lives takes much more intentionality. We know that God is behind it if our children do anything well. There is no goodness in any of us without His grace.

Time to Parent

These five steps will biblically position you to critique your children:

1. **STEP 1:** Catch your child doing something good.
2. **STEP 2:** Isolate the attitude, word, or action.
3. **STEP 3:** Identify it by connecting it to something Jesus would have done.
4. **STEP 4:** Encourage your child by letting him know he got it right. He needs your encouragement and to know that his actions are Christlike.
5. **STEP 5:** Perchance, you must critique your child, your love will swallow up the disappointment because of your constant and overwhelming love that he knows you have for him.

Day 14

Love Your Children Just 'Cause

For by grace, you have been saved through faith. And this is not your own doing; it is the gift of God, not a result of works, so that no one may boast.
(Ephesians 2:8-9)

One of the most practical things a parent could do for their children is to love them just because it is God-like. You don't need a reason other than they are your kids. God loves you that way. He loves you just because you're His child.

The Lord does not come to you saying, "If you clean your room, I will love you today." Or, "If you make straight A's, I will love you." He does not place conditions or requirements on His love for you. He loves you when you do well, and He loves you when you fail. He is crazy in love with you not because of your works but because you placed your faith in the works of His Son. There are no levels of righteousness with God. There is only one level, which is the perfect level that only Christ could reach. Relating to God is unlike a cosmic arcade game where the higher the level you ascend, the greater the reward you receive. It's not like the harder you work for God's affection, the more love He will give to you. The Son of God already hit the highest possible level. Jesus gave the perfect sacrifice on the cross, which was entirely satisfying to His Father.

There is only one thing for you to do: accept the Son's works and live in the freedom of the Father's love. That is the kind of parental love you want to give to your children. Walk up to your young son, rub his head, and tell him that you love him just because. If he is an older child, you may want to do something like hug him. How about squeezing your daughter's hand and telling her you love her? If she asks, "Why?" Say, "Just 'cause. Just because you're my daughter, I thank God for giving you to me. You are a gift to me, and I appreciate you." Let them know you love them often and without an expectation that they must meet your preferred requirements. There are other times when you can talk about holiness, obedience, and following Jesus. Today, love them without tying your affections to expectations of performance. If you want to blow their minds, show them your love just moments after they disappoint you.

Sin moments are fantastic times to reaffirm your love for them. Surprise them with grace, which is always better than yelling at them as you remind them what a disappointment they are to you. Grace is how your Father treats you. It feels good. It motivates you to love Him in return. I'm not saying you should not deal with their sin, but part of dealing with a person's sin is making sure they know you're crazy in love with them. Are you crazy in love with your children? Do they know you're crazy in love with them? Is there any hint in their hearts to perform for you because you have put that thought in their minds? It's one thing for them to feel like they need to please you because of their Adamic natures, but it's horrible if a parent motivates them to be people pleasers.

Time to Parent

1. Do not make your children work for your affection. It will not go well for them today or as adults if you make them work for your love.
2. Have they picked up on subtle messages that you will be happy with them if they perform a certain way?
3. What specific way do you need to change?

Day 15

Discipline Comes from Love

> My Son, do not despise the LORD's discipline or be weary of his reproof, for the LORD reproves him whom he loves, as a father the Son in whom he delights.
>
> (Proverbs 3:11-12)

How do you discipline your children? What if I asked the question from your child's perspective? What is their experience with your corrective care? Biblical restorative care always begins with God. You want to imitate the Father, especially regarding discipline (Ephesians 5:1).

In the text, you see that the Father disciplines from a heart of love. How could He not? God is love (1 John 4:8). When you experience His discipline, you are experiencing corrective care from a loving person. Your children experience who you are, too—whether you're a loving person or an unloving person. If you are motivated and managed by love, your kids will feel your corrective care from a loving person, which will make your discipline redemptive. Because you are a loving person, your discipline will not be the first time you engaged your child in loving ways. God has a long and loving relational history with you. I cannot overstate the importance of this. If your love does not predate your time of discipline, you will confuse and frustrate your child.

Here are four compelling and convincing ways you have experienced the Father's love:

- He predetermined His love for you (Ephesians 1:4-5).
- He loved you enough to give you His Son as a ransom (John 3:16).
- His Son gave His life for you, though you did not deserve it (Romans 5:8).
- His Spirit came to bring you daily comfort and guidance (John 16:13).

The point is that you had experienced the Father's love many times before you experienced His discipline. He was putting money in the bank long before He took any out. That's why His withdrawals do not hurt like they would if you were a bankrupt child. Suppose you went to your local bank to make a withdrawal. Upon arriving at your local bank, you discover that you have no money in the bank. You're broke. Let's turn the illustration around. Suppose you have been steadily putting cash in your local bank–every week of your life. You then go to the bank to make a withdrawal. Even though you prefer not to take money out of the bank, you know it's possible, and when it's necessary to pay a debt, you make the withdrawal. It stings a bit but does not deplete your account or spirit. Your weekly deposits have made it possible for you to take money out when it's necessary.

Practically letting your child know that you love him is putting money in the bank. And why wouldn't you do this? The doctrine of sin informs you that there will be times when you will have to make disciplinary withdrawals; your child is not perfect. He needs your corrective and restorative care. The onus is on you to be intentional in making sure that you have convinced your child that you love him. If you do not do this daily, you will tempt your child to give up on the relationship—once he figures out how and when to do it. It will begin with quiet disrespect. After your child becomes a teen, his disregard for you will be more blatant. He will give you the finger in his heart; later, he will be bolder. The behavior you hoped for him will morph into rebellion.

Time to Parent

1. What do your children experience more from you: your correction or your encouragement?
2. Prayerfully consider this devotional. If you need to talk to a trusted friend, please do not delay—do it today.

Day 16

The Wisdom of Engaging the Sin

If we say we have no sin, we deceive ourselves, and the truth is not in us. If we confess our sins, he is faithful and just to forgive us our sins and to cleanse us from all unrighteousness. If we say we have not sinned, we make him a liar, and his word is not in us.

(1 John 1:8-10)

A family with a gospel-centered view of sin experiences something that never crosses the mind of their culture. Once you tap into God's grace at this level, sin is not a disadvantage but an opportunity to magnify God through your family's imperfections. Here is a short list of those advantages.

- You confess your sins.
- You receive forgiveness.
- You reconcile with God and each other.
- You enjoy restoration with others.
- You overcome sin.
- You model the gospel life.
- You teach others these gospel benefits.
- You enjoy honest and vulnerable relationships.

What a great list, and it's for you. I talk to parents regularly who are doing these things, and it is such an encouragement to hear their stories of grace about God's faithfulness, primarily when sin seeks to destroy them. Of course, the opposite is also true. If you don't practically live in the gospel's power, the engagement of sin in your family will be disastrous. Here are a few of those adverse effects.

- **INSECURITY:** Your children will experience your sinfulness, and it will hurt them. They will look for safety through other people and means that are outside your home.
- **ANGER:** They may walk away from God because they perceive your Christianity as a method to keep them out of trouble. It has no real impact on your life. They will also resent you.
- **DISHONESTY:** By not owning your sin, you essentially say that sin does not matter. The truth is, it does exist, and it does matter. Your children will react to your lack of integrity about your sin.
- **SELF-RIGHTEOUSNESS:** Your kids will not have the equipping to work through relational conflict. As adults, when sin happens in their relationships, instead of repenting, they may choose a similar self-righteous path of justifying, rationalizing, or blaming their sin on other people or events.
- **LICENTIOUSNESS:** Individuals who do not gain victory over sin succumb to the temptation to sin more as a response. They spin in a frustrating sin cycle. If sin is not exposed or discussed, and the family is not walking out repentance, you can guarantee more sin.
- **DISQUALIFIED:** Your children will resent you and not listen to your counsel, even when you are right. Your lack of honesty will influence their perspective of you, which will functionally disqualify you as a parent.

The death of Christ loudly proclaims everyone is a sinner. No Christian should hide this fact behind a wall of hypocrisy. To reject the reality of sin is to deny the gospel. One of the kindest things you can do is learn how to engage the sin in your family so they can enjoy the full benefits of the gospel. Let your family see how you may be ashamed of your sin but not of the gospel. Help release your children from the sin that hopes to trap them. You can do this if you humble yourself before God and your family and let them see the advantage of engaging sin with the gospel.

Time to Parent

Every family has a sin plan because sin is in every family. Some sin plans are uninformed biblically.

1. What is your sin plan?
2. Do you have a redemptive sin plan for yourself and your family?
3. What does a biblical sin plan that includes confession, forgiveness, reconciliation, restoration, and ongoing engagement with future sin look like in your home?

Day 17

Introducing the World

Train up a child in the way he should go; even when he is old he will not depart from it.

(Proverbs 22:6)

The little people in your home will only be in your home for a nano-second. They may spend ninety percent of their lives outside of your parental jurisdiction. It is wise to equip them to live well in the world that will make up nearly all of their earthly existence. Appropriately introducing them to their future culture will benefit them today and tomorrow.

When I say introducing your child to the world, I am not talking about teaching them how to curse, drink beer, watch porn, smoke cigarettes, and do other sin-festive things that our culture loves. I am speaking about familiarizing your child with the world's ways while also teaching him how not to imbibe. You do not want your kids to be surprised, repulsed, or tempted by the things in our culture when they enter into it as young adults. If you don't teach them today how to engage the world before they are adults, they will be like a child reaching for a hot stove because he did not know it was hot. And your child will be burned by the culture that you so meticulously kept away from him. Your home is a laboratory. You should be continually challenging your kids so you can understand them better.

If you have more than one child, you know about their uniqueness, which is why you cannot do cookie-cutter parenting. For example, to say that alcohol is evil and you'll go to hell if you drink it is fear-motivated parental ignorance. While you may bind the conscience of one child, and he treats alcohol like a plague all of his life, your next child may not be so motivated. Children need loving and wise instruction, not fear tactics. Sheltering is an integral part of parenting, without question. Parents understand this, but sheltering and fear-based protection should never be the beginning and the end of your child's life. If it is, your kids will be culturally confused and spiritually tempted when their time comes to stand without your guidance. It may seem wise (and convenient) to shelter your children, but if you do, beware: you won't know them how you need to during this training season.

It's better to create those testing opportunities—with instruction—while they are with you rather than waiting for them to leave you and flounder in their culture. One of the ways we have equipped our children for the future is by connecting them with adults. They have been socializing with adults ever since they could socialize as toddlers. We strategically and appropriately gave them a few adults to play with while they were young. Like all children, they naturally gravitate to their kind. Like fish to water, they love other kids. We had to be intentional in connecting them with older, bigger, and wiser people. Small groups in the local church are safe places for this kind of adult training. Hospitality in the home is also an excellent context. There are other ways to bring the world into your laboratory so you can teach your children.

We opened bank accounts when our kids were approximately five years old and started teaching them Systematic Theology at that age. When they were about eight years old, we watched specific Cops episodes (a

TV Show) to teach them to respect police officers while introducing them to the drug and alcohol culture. During the sex talk season, I began teaching them some of the culture's language. There are many other ways to introduce them to their futures incrementally.

Time to Parent

1. Do you give blanket edicts to your kids, not considering their uniqueness?
2. How are you customizing your parenting to each of your children?

Day 18

Teaching Children Curse Words

Let the words of my mouth and the meditation of my heart be acceptable in your sight, O LORD, my rock and my redeemer.

(Psalm 19:14)

It is impossible to engage our culture at any level and not hear curse words. Whether it is a television show or a stroll in the park, the words of our culture do not discriminate. They do not care who you are. Every caring parent must answer the question, "Who is going to teach my child the culture's language?"

This training begins with a transcending and overarching parenting goal: to love God and others as you love yourself (Matthew 22:36-40). As your child learns this unique two-tiered worldview about loving God and others, you can begin laying down a sound language strategy that will consist of three parts:

1. Teach your child what God's Word says (or implies) about language.
2. Test your child on how he uses language in relational contexts.
3. Incrementally release your child into the world to use language redemptively.

With a God-loving, other-centered worldview in place, you can instruct your child to rise above the unedifying noise of our culture. Your leadership wisdom knows better than to turn language training over to someone who does not believe the way you do. You want your children to learn the words of our culture, what the words mean, and how and when to use the world's language.

Using words correctly and biblically takes more maturity than using them harmfully. You can walk through any crowded public venue and hear that people do not know how to use words redemptively. They know words but do not know how to use them to build up others, motivating any parent to take the lead in language learning. Your children will not always watch G and PG movies or permanently live in a G and PG world. Your hope is when the world comes knocking, your kids won't be vulnerable to its temptations but will be able to intelligently, humbly, and courageously engage their culture.

Time to Parent

These six tips will help you as you instruct your child. But before you can teach your child, you want to assess your use of words. These tips start with you.

1. **REFRAIN FROM BEING HUNG UP ABOUT WORDS.** Words are words. You do not have to giggle when you say penis or feel like you've gotten away with something when you say damn. The more significant issue is the motive behind your words (Luke 6:45).

2. **CONSIDER YOUR AUDIENCE.** Do your words uplift and build up or degrade and tear down? The gospel is more about others than about you. Always think of others. Never use your freedom as a right to do as you please.

3. **WHAT IS YOUR MOTIVE?** Make sure your heart is saturated by the gospel when you speak. Let the words of your mouth come from a heart treasure informed by the gospel. If so, your speech will be redemptive.

4. **ARE YOU A CRUDE DUDE?** Regularly assess yourself. What has the feedback been from those closest to you? How do they perceive, understand, and think about your speech patterns?

5. **HAVE YOUR WORDS WEIGHED.** Most people will not give honest and critical feedback about the more profound matters of the heart. You will have to pursue it. Feel free to seek out your friends to serve you with their assessment of your speech patterns.

6. **ARE YOU AN ENCOURAGER?** Do the people around you feel more encouraged or discouraged after spending time with you? How does your speech affect others? Are you characterized as a redemptive builder by your words? Please explain.

Day 19

If You Could Export One Thing

By faith, he left Egypt, not being afraid of the anger of the king, for he endured as seeing him who is invisible.

(Hebrews 11:27)

After all these years of counseling and all the trouble I've seen in people's lives, it has become more real to me than ever how we need a better worldview and foundation on which to land when we fall. Learning how to fall well is God's mercy to us. God is the only person who can accurately answer the why question after you fall. The Lord is your best answer when trouble comes, and if you do not know Him well, your suffering will be more complicated than it needs to be.

The most oft-repeated appeal in the Bible, either explicit or implied, is "fear not." The Lord is always calling His people to trust Him. You cannot fully trust someone you do not know, which is your call to elevate your theology—the study of God—above all else. If we could export one thing to our children, we would choose theology as the main thing, which is what we did when they were younger. We wanted them to walk into their adult lives knowing God, and out of that knowledge, our hope was for them to enjoy every good thing the Bible offers to theologically-centered Godlovers. If they don't have sound theology—understanding God—what will grow out of their lives will not be the best it could be. I'm not talking about having Bible knowledge, as in knowing the facts of the Bible. I'm talking about knowing God.

- If they are going to have strong faith, they must know God well.
- If they are going to live practical lives, they must know God.
- If they are going to love others the right way, they must know God correctly.

We wanted our children to know the Lord, His person, character, attributes, and all the things He can do. We hoped that when real-life problems confront them, they could endure them because they could perceive their great invisible God. Thus, we spent a lot of time teaching our children a sound theology. Here is a list of some of the terms that we taught them when they were young. The list goes from left to right as it moves through a sequence of who God is and what He does for His children. They first learned the term theology as they became theologians. Then, they began learning about God.

Theology	Theologian	Polytheism
Trinity	Sovereignty	Omnipotent
Omniscience	Omnipresence	Transcendence
Holy	Immutable	Hypostatic Union
Redeemer	Resurrection	Gospel
The Fall	Depravity	Sin

Idolatry	Regeneration	Adoption
Justification	Sanctification	Repentance
Worship		

The weakness of too many Christians is their need for more theological depth. Nobody taught them theology; their parents didn't teach them; their youth groups didn't instruct them. They were actively part of a church but not practically engaging in theology. Some parents and youth leaders seem to have a theological timidity as if children are too ignorant, immature, or disinterested to learn theological truths about God. It's not true. Our kids were encouraged and motivated when the big people in the room let them into their adult world of big words like the hypostatic union. They perceived our respect, love, care for, and trust in them, which created an eagerness in them to learn more about God. The problem was not their lack of capacity to learn but our lack of awareness regarding the opportunity before us and the lack of intentionality to step into that opportunity.

Time to Parent

1. Give your children a good view of who God is and what He can do. They need to know Him more than they need to know anything else in life, and from that foundation, you can equip them with all of the other things they will need to know to be mature, God-loving adults.

Day 20

Dangerous Pragmatic Parenting

Love is patient and kind.

(1 Corinthians 13:4)

Pragmatic parenting is a rule-based, heavily structured, and self-reliant methodology. Some of the family rules are good and biblical, while others are based on preferences and conveniences. It's an unwise parenting model.

Have you met the counting lady? Let's call her Mable. Maybe you have seen her in Walmart, standing in the checkout line. Her 7-year-old son—let's call him Biffy—was disobeying her, and she was fearfully hoping he would stop being disruptive. Her method for getting little Biffy to behave was to count. 1... 2... 3 .... This method is like a game of dare. Mable begins a slow cadence down a dead-end street, hoping Biffy will get a clue and choose respect and obedience. This method is often the product of a fearful or angry heart.

- Fearful because Mable is embarrassed by what others may think of her.
- Angry because she is frustrated with little Biffy.

She may stop counting and start yelling if he does not respond favorably. She may grab a body part to motivate him to cease misbehaving. She will be at a loss if her method becomes punitive and he does not respond correctly. Success in Mable's mind is an immediate behavioral modification, whether it comes through anger, the infliction of pain, or the threat of future retribution from Biffy's dad after he arrives home. The sad thing for Biffy is that he will not be transformed from the inside out because the parenting model is pragmatic—immediate behavioral results—rather than centered on gospel truths. If there is shalom in their home, it will be temporary because the transformation comes through manipulation out of fear or anger. In many of these situations, the dad has not been leading the family. He may not be in the picture or have delegated his parental role to his wife because he is preoccupied with more important things like his job.

Part of the parent's motivation is to keep their child from becoming whatever it is they fear. This "something" is usually part of the parent's experience. Rather than trusting God by parenting from the Bible, they oversteer the car, choosing to parent from anxious fear. If your parenting is not connected to and does not flow from the gospel, you will set up your children for current frustration and future failure. Many pragmatically parented children spend their adult lives un-parenting themselves. They have to unlearn their parents' negative shaping influences. If you believe you are a pragmatic parent, the first thing to do is examine your parenting worldview. Do you know how to parent according to the gospel? What is your methodology for cooperating with God in the transformation of your child? Do you primarily parent the way the Lord parents you? A biblical diagnostic that will help you examine your parenting style is 1 Corinthians 13:4-7. Read and insert your name into each blank where the word love is explicit or implied in the Bible text.

_____ is patient	_____ is kind
_____ does not envy	_____ does not boast
_____ is not arrogant	_____ is not rude
_____ doesn't insist on way	_____ is not irritable
_____ is not resentful	_____ rejoice not in wrong
_____ rejoices with truth	_____ bears all things
_____ believes all things	_____ hopes all things
_____ endures all things	

Time to Parent

1. If you need to change your parenting strategy, a perfect place to begin is to identify the weaknesses that the diagnostic revealed. It would be profitable to have a friend walk with you through the process as you take your soul to task regarding each of the descriptors the Spirit has revealed to you as an area of needed improvement.

Day 21

Two Acceptable Conflicts

The saying is trustworthy and deserving of full acceptance, that Christ Jesus came into the world to save sinners, of whom I am the foremost.

(1 Timothy 1:15)

For even the Son of Man came not to be served but to serve, and to give his life as a ransom for many.

(Mark 10:45)

Two people can't agree on everything completely. If you are married, you know this is true. Two fallen people living in proximity to each other will always have a few perspectives and preferences that will never be the same. It is unavoidable, and it does not have to be a bad thing. What if you had unresolvable good conflict in your family? Are there some things to which you should never agree? In our family, we have narrowed our good conflicts down to two things we will never agree on.

The Biggest Sinner

Who is the greatest sinner in your home? Paul said he was the foremost sinner, but he died, leaving a vacancy in the chief sinner seat. The answer to the biggest sinner question is easy to figure out from my perspective. There is no sin worse than being accused of putting the Son of God to death on a cross. From my point of view and through my eyes, there is no question that I am the chief sinner. We have discussed this many times as a family, and none of us have reached a resolution other than disagreeing. Lucia believes she is the biggest sinner in our home.

I suspect if Paul were here, he would chime in by saying he was the chief of sinners. As our children grew older, they began to see how Lucia and I were wrong. Why should something so simple be so complicated? Though we will never agree, there is an upside: it's hard to get into arguments when everyone in the room assumes the role of the chief sinner. The other upside is that after you blow it, you're quicker to repent and reconcile with each other. And honestly, it is not wrong to view others through the lens of the cross. As you realize the debt God paid for your sin, it becomes easier to show mercy to others.

> And should not you have had mercy on your fellow servant, as I had mercy on you?
>
> (Matthew 18:33)

The Biggest Servant

What naturally flows out of an acute awareness that you put Christ on the cross is a humility that leads to action. Just as it becomes challenging to be sinful toward another person, it is a natural reflex to want to serve those within your sphere of influence. The person who sees himself as the biggest sinner, made alive and saved by God (Ephesians 2:1-10), is motivated to respond to that grace by serving others. Serving others is foundational to understanding the gospel. Christ came to serve, not to be served (Mark 10:45), creating a conflict in our home. Nobody is permitted to out-serve the other person.

Outdo one another in showing honor.

(Romans 12:10)

The gospel is not for the lazy person. It is a call to take your soul to task while motivating yourself to work for others. The anti-gospel sees others as worse than yourself while using them for self-serving purposes.

Time to Parent

1. From your point of view, who is the biggest sinner in your home? This theological tip is a transformative relational dynamic if you genuinely believe as Paul did.
2. Who is the most aggressive servant in your home?
3. If you think you're better than others, you won't serve others. If you're not serving others, you believe you're better than others.

Day 22

Tips from the Best Parent

Therefore be imitators of God, as beloved children.
(Ephesians 5:1)

The best way to learn how to be the best parent is to learn from the best parent. God, the Father, is the best parent the world has ever known. Understanding and applying His parenting to your family is one of the wisest things you can do.

Knowing God and imitating God are two different things. The demons know about God, but they do not follow Him (James 2:19) because they do not exercise biblical faith. Biblical faith has three parts: knowledge, understanding, and practice. The last one—practice—is what makes faith biblical. If your faith is not authentically activated, it's not biblical faith. A Christian's faith is Christlike. I have five tips to help you flesh out what it means to look like Jesus to your family. You can immediately implement these characteristics into your home. Along with each tip are application questions that will aid you in this opportunity to imitate God the Father for your children.

MODEL: *God Is an Example:* Christ's life was the example of what you are to become; similarly, what you model before your children will have a lifetime impact on them (Ephesians 5:1).

1. What are you modeling before your kids?
2. Is your religion exportable? As a missionary to your family, you are exporting the life of Christ to them. Are they receiving what you are exporting?
3. What would happen if your children made copious notes of your life and imitated what they observed from you (Philippians 4:9)?

HONEST: *God Is Honest:* The Father is honest with you because He is the truth (John 14:6). Leading your children by being open with them is one of the ways you can honor God.

1. When was the last time you confessed your sin to your child?
2. When was the last time you asked your child to forgive you?
3. Do you respond to all of the sins in your home equally in terms of transparency, vulnerability, forgiveness, confession, and reconciliation?

ENCOURAGE: *God Is an Encourager:* The Father uses kindness as a means to motivate you to change (Romans 2:4). It is His great love for you (John 3:16) that transforms you (Romans 12:1-2).

1. What was the last specific way you encouraged your child?
2. Is your child more aware of your pleasure or displeasure in him?
3. How often did you encourage your child today? This week? If you have not encouraged your child lately, you have something special to look forward to today.

SERVE: *God Is a Servant:* Christ is the epitome of servanthood. One of His purposes for coming to earth was to serve you, which is at the heart of the gospel (Mark 10:45).

1. Would you consider your home an other-centered home?
2. How are you regularly serving your children?
3. Does your family have peripheral vision? This concept means they quickly see the needs of the home and are eager to do it.

A portion of this kind of serving includes acts of sanctification like confession, honesty, forgiveness, kindness, encouragement, motivation, and humility. Biblically serving your family is more than washing dishes; it's active repentance, too.

LOVE: *God Is Love:* Love is an action word. The Lord is the ultimate action Lover. He is not distant or passive regarding His children (John 1:14).

1. Do you take the time to meaningfully engage your kids? Do you proactively plan time with your spouse and children in mind?
2. Do you relate to your spouse in a way that you want your kids to relate to each other?
3. Practically speaking, what does your love look like toward your spouse and your children?

Day 23

I Failed As a Parent

Whatever the LORD pleases, he does, in heaven and on earth, in the seas and all deeps.

(Psalm 135:6)

Parents love and care for their children, which is a good thing. Some parents over-care for their children, which is challenging, especially when their kids are not walking with the Lord. Many of these parents struggle as they rehearse how they failed their children.

Anytime there is parent/child conflict, the first place to assess the situation is always with the plank in your eye (Matthew 7:3-5). But after repentance, you must move past the failures. If you don't, you will make them worse. It is instructive when a parent does not leave their parenting sins with Jesus (1 John 1:9). The biggest problem with staying stuck on parenting failure is the self-centered nature of it. The parent becomes the plaintiff, prosecuting attorney, and judge of the child's problems.

- **PLAINTIFF:** You lodge a case against yourself.
- **PROSECUTING ATTORNEY:** you bring up all the reasons for a conviction against yourself.
- **JUDGE:** you listen to the arguments, nod in agreement, and condemn yourself.

Self-centered complaining and condemnation are godless, hermetically sealed, closed systems that do not account for God's sovereign care in your life and do not allow the Lord to be part of the situation. A stuck parent in regret is a call to re-index the heart back to the gospel. Most people will say "yes and amen" to reorienting their minds to the goodness and freedom found in the gospel, but doing it is challenging. If your child makes mistakes, you must answer what went wrong, including more than failed parenting. One of those other things is that God is permitting your child's mistakes to happen. Yes, God is in your child's mistakes. How could an omnipresent, omnipotent, and omniscient God do otherwise? You will not be free from the failed parenting mantra in your head until you acknowledge, accept, and rest in God's role in your child's life.

Parents who blame themselves perpetually for their child's failure are not trusting God the way they should. They are stuck with no remedy, so they blame themselves for what's wrong. Rather than focusing blame on yourself or your child, it would be wiser to understand God's role in your family's problems. This process begins by letting go of what you want for your child—according to your expectations and resolved according to your timetable. As long as you refuse to let go of your dreams and desires for your child, no matter how biblical they may sound, you will always be in bondage to their failures. Your slavery will take on many forms, like blame, despair, criticalness, depression, bitterness, hopelessness, frustration, and confusion. The first question you want to examine is what's happening in your heart. What is it that keeps a vice grip on your heart? The obvious answer is unbelief: you are not trusting God functionally.

You may be a believer, but from a functional perspective, you're an untrusting one. Ironically, your child's unwillingness to trust God reveals a heart of unbelief in you, which is a mercy from the Lord that He would use your child to help you draw closer to Him. As you address your heart of unbelief, you must next release your child from your expectations. If you attempt to over-protect your child from failure, you will be an accomplice in the child's failures.

Time to Parent

1. Job said, "The Lord gives, and the Lord takes away. Blessed be the name of the Lord" (Job 1:21). How do you need to change to bless the Lord regardless of what He permits into your life?

Day 24

Consider Stop Parenting

What you have learned and received and heard and seen in me—practice these things, and the God of peace will be with you.

(Philippians 4:9)

You cannot create unity from disunity. What is on the inside will come out on the outside. If disunity is in your marriage, disunity will flow out of it. If disunity characterizes your marriage, the likelihood of your children being relationally dysfunctional is strong.

Think about it this way. What if there was division in the Trinity? What if the Father, Son, and Spirit were angry with each other? If it were true, we would not stand a chance of being loved or protected well. Mercifully, we do not have to worry about whether the Godhead will stay together or if they will get into a yelling match. Have you ever worried that way about them? I suspect it has never crossed your mind, or if it did, it was a fleeting thought that you immediately shrugged off as impossible. God's children do not worry about the stability of the Godhead, and your kids should not have to worry about the stability of their parents. You should not put that kind of burden on them. When your children think about your marriage, they should immediately think about love, joy, peace, patience, kindness, and the other manifestations of the fruit of the Spirit (Galatians 5:22-23).

Suppose your children are more aware of your marriage's hostility, unforgiveness, and general disunity. In that case, their hearts will be motivated to gravitate toward more stable and secure things—from their immature perspectives. Everybody wants security; nobody likes instability. When I was a teen, I found my stability through my ability to perform well at my job. My work gave me the things I craved, things my parents would not give me because of their unwillingness to love each other well and, out of that love, to love me well.

Security, approval, acceptance, and a sense of accomplishment were mine to have as long as I could perform for my employer. And I did. My work was my refuge. My home was a chaotic context for disunity. Homelife was something to endure, while my job experience was a pleasurable escape. This course of action is natural for teenagers who live in chaotic homes. Their hearts drift to something they can control—something that will not disappoint them. All of us have a desire to look for love. Too often, we find this love in the wrong places.

I suspect some parents read this and think they cause their children's rejection of the Lord. Other parents might believe their children will follow Jesus because they are good parents. Both opinions are wrong. Good parents do not make Christians, and neither do bad parents. A Christian is made a Christian because of the gospel, and the gospel comes to individuals because of the Lord's unmerited favor (Ephesians 2:8-9). Do not fall into the trap of, "What have I done to my children?"

But you must give biblical reflection to, "What have I done to my kids," especially if your marriage does not represent Christ and His church (Ephesians 5:25). Two ditches exist here, and you do not want to fall into either one. The self-righteous person will think their works matter. The arrogant individual will presume on the grace of God (Psalm 19:13).

Time to Parent

1. Is your marriage hindering your children from loving Jesus?
2. What are some of the attitudes or actions in your marriage that you need to change so you can more effectively put Christ on display in your home?
3. Even if your spouse does not cooperate, how should you change?

Day 25

A Secret Weapon to Motivate

Do you presume on the riches of his kindness and forbearance and patience, not knowing that God's kindness is meant to lead you to repentance?

(Romans 2:4)

When you think about your heavenly Father, you are immediately aware of His kindness, patience, forbearance, and affection for you. These thoughts about your heavenly Father are strikingly fundamental because how He treats you is how you are to treat others, especially your children. Scores of verses in the New Testament teach about God's amazing love for us. As you read these verses, consider how God's unquenching love motivates you toward change.

- He loved you while you were a sinner (Romans 5:8).
- He loves you even when He disciplines you (Hebrews 12:6).
- He gave His life for you (Hebrews 12:2; 1 Corinthians 6:20).
- He is entirely and undeniably on your side (Romans 8:31-34).
- He healed you from your sin by taking your sin upon Himself (1 Peter 2:24; 2 Corinthians 5:21).
- He secures you by His mighty power (John 10:28-30).

Don't these gospel truths motivate you toward Christian maturity? Doesn't this kind of aggressive love inspire you to change? God's unmerited favor was the critical point Paul was making to the Romans when he began to give them a gospel-centered perspective on how people change in Romans 2:4. In context, Paul had just turned his argument for the need to change from the pagan Gentiles (Romans 1:16-32) to the Jews (Romans 2:1). He told his ethnic brothers the same kindness, forbearance, and patience the Father showed to the Gentiles is also being offered to them.

He did not want them to presume on—take for granted— God's kindness, knowing it is God's kindness that leads to change. How repentance happens is essential knowledge as you think about how it works in your child's life. If your home is not a context of kindness, where your kids are knowing and experiencing your love, don't be surprised if authentic change does not come to them. I'm talking about the love of God practically displayed and given to your children. The gospel-discerning parent can do this because kindness begets kindness.

A good tree will produce good fruit (Luke 6:44-45). If you are living in and experiencing the daily love of God (root/ heart), you can produce the love of God (fruit/actions) toward others. You can only give what you possess. You will exasperate them if you do not have genuine affection for your children and if you're not regularly showing that kindness. Loving well takes work. Gospel work is never easy because gospel work is always other-centered.

Time to Parent

How do you think you score with your children? What do your kids think about when they think about you? Let's put these questions into two categories: affection and gratitude and correction and displeasure. Here are some practical questions you can ask your children:

1. When you think of me, do you first think of my love and affection for you, or do you think more about my displeasure and correction of you?
2. What do you think first when I say I have something to say to you? Am I going to encourage you, or will I discourage you?
3. Do you consider me to be a joy to be around, or do you consider me more of a burden to be around?
4. If you could choose a word that best describes my affection (or lack thereof) for you, what would that word be?

Think of these questions as conversation starters that will allow you to engage your children in a tangible way that does not pressure them to change.

Day 26

The Perfect Goal

Him we proclaim, warning everyone and teaching everyone with all wisdom, that we may present everyone mature in Christ.

(Colossians 1:28)

What do you hope your child will be after he grows up? Many Christians would say they wish their child loved God and others as he loves himself (Matthew 22:36-40). Those are two great goals, but what do they mean?

If you told your child that you wanted him to love God and others as much as he loves himself, what would he hear? Would he know what to do? Maybe the better question is, how are you training him to accomplish the goal of loving God and loving others? We wanted to implement the Matthew 22:36-40 plan into our children to help them think practically about it. When our kids were younger, they knew they were supposed to love God and others as they loved themselves, but they didn't understand what it practically meant to live that kind of life. Not practically living the two great commandments raises an important point: kids must learn more than Bible facts. Knowing and living the Bible are radically different things, though both pieces are needed to be mature. Knowledge only was one of the rebukes Paul leveled on the Corinthians. You see it in 1 Corinthians 8:1-2. He acknowledged that they had Bible knowledge. Knowing theology was not the issue that Paul had with the Corinthians. His rebuke was their inability (or lack of awareness) to apply the Bible to their lives.

He taught how stand-alone-Bible-knowledge led to arrogance. He warned them about this when he said, "knowledge puffs up, but love builds up." He began teaching them how to apply the Bible so their brothers would not trip up over the meat-eating problem they had with the Jews who had just become Christians. He taught that mature Christians were not just Bible-smart but practically equipped. A helpful equation is Knowledge + Application = Wisdom. Wisdom is the ability to apply the knowledge of the Bible in practical ways that make sense. If you know only, there will be a temptation to be arrogant. If you have an application without knowledge, you will stumble into subjective weirdness.

Suppose you have a clear understanding of the Bible and can bring practical application of the Bible to your life and the lives of others. In that case, you'll experience wisdom, which is biblical maturity. There are a lot of intelligent Bible people walking around our world today, and many biblically illiterate individuals are subjectively applying the Bible in ways the biblical writers never intended. We need students of the Word of God who know how to practically apply the Word of God to their lives and their culture. What the world needs are mature adults, and that is the goal for our children. To be more specific, we want them to be relationally mature Christians.

- We want them to have a relationally mature life with Christ.
- We want them to have a relationally mature life with others.

That is how we thought about practicalizing Matthew 22:36-40 into their lives. Think about it with me. What are some of the more significant problems you see in yourself and others? If you could use a word, I think immaturity would be a good one.

- Immature people stay angry.
- Immature people are self-serving.
- Immature people are discontented.
- Immature people hide behind masks.

Time to Parent

1. How are you training your child in Bible knowledge and the practical application of that knowledge?
2. Christian maturity provides an answer for all of these things, plus much more. If you need additional help, go through this devotional series as often as you need to until you practically live out the truths in the milieu of your life.

Day 27

When All You Do Is Correct

Commit your work to the LORD, and your plans will be established.

(Proverbs 16:3)

When your children are young, it can seem that all you're doing is correcting them. As soon as they begin walking upright and stringing syllables together, there appears to be no right or wrong that they cannot do or say. Parents can quickly find themselves saying, "No," "Stop," "Don't," and "Stop talking" at every turn of their day. Though the parent knows she should encourage her child more than correct him, it seems that the rapidity with which he makes mistakes leaves no time for positive affirmation. When the problems outnumber the good things your child does, here are fifteen ideas that will help you.

1. Don't sweat the small stuff. Overlook as much as you can. Choose only a handful of things you will bring to your child's attention.
2. Discern the episodes and patterns. If the mistakes are not part of an ongoing pattern in your child's life, you can probably overlook them. Spend more time correcting patterns.
3. Look for the presence of goodness, not its

perfection. Your goal is not a perfect five-year-old. You want to discern the presence of good qualities that you hope will flourish when the child is older.

4. Work hard at encouraging. If he is often sinning, work twice as hard at finding evidence of God's grace in his life so you can encourage him.

5. Don't undervalue "Thank you." When you see him doing the right things, say "thank you," no matter how small or seemingly insignificant that something may appear.

6. You're not the mini-messiah. God changes individuals; you do not. You'll know if you're the mini-messiah when your worry or frustration is more significant than your rest in the Lord.

7. Don't take a poll of your parenting. If you ask an immature, self-centered child if you're critical, the data will probably return in the affirmative. Ask the Lord how you're doing, and maybe a close friend who knows you.

8. Don't be the judge and jury of your parenting. Remember that God can use sin sinlessly. You don't want to sin, but trust the Sovereign God when you do.

9. Commit your parenting to the Lord. You are parenting for God's fame most of all. Don't be a results-oriented parent, or you'll stress over every perceived failure.

10. Failures are opportunities. When things don't go according to your plans, ask the Lord how you can learn from what just happened.

11. Don't compare yourself with others. Paul said those who compare themselves among themselves are not wise (2 Corinthians 10:12). Don't be unwise. You're not omniscient; you do not know everything about those you're comparing with yourself.

12. Paint a picture of Jesus. In addition to all these

active things, passively live the life of Jesus before your child. Let him see what Christ looks like, especially when you're having a bad day. You can find nine portraits of Jesus in Galatians 5:22-23.

13. Know your audience. As the Lord told Samuel (paraphrased), your son is not rejecting you; he is rejecting the Lord from being his authority (1 Samuel 8:7). Stay focused on what's going on with your child.

14. Make discipline short. When it's time to correct your child, do not drag it out for hours. Make it short, memorable, and redemptive. Extend your praise and shorten your discipline.

15. Talk during non-fight times. When there is no conflict, it's best to discuss what's happening in your child's heart.

Time to Parent

1. Discuss these fifteen ideas with a close friend and plan to revisit them until you master them.

Day 28

To Have Fantastic Children

Trust in the LORD with all your heart, and do not lean on your own understanding. In all your ways acknowledge him, and he will make straight your paths.

(Proverbs 3:5-6)

Every loving parent wants their children to turn out well. However, they are also aware they have a role to play. Though God is the primary change agent, parents are secondary agents who must cooperate with the Lord to transform their children. Here are seven tips to help those parents.

1. **PRAYING:** While this is an expected tip, it is at the top of the list because God is the only person who can change anyone (2 Timothy 2:24-25). If you want your child to change, you must plead with the Lord to change him. If your child does transform, God did it. If he does not, the Lord has not (at this point) granted repentance. There is a mystery here that you must fully engage. On your best day, all you can do is water and plant. God is the one who brings growth to a person's life.

2. **BEING:** Your life must always be imitating God. Your child needs to see an authentic Christlike life. You are "Exhibit A" to that life. The best role you can play in your child's life is to give him an authentic life that includes your mistakes. Your mistakes may be the most informative way to teach your child the Christ life. After you fail, you have an incredible opportunity to model how to respond to failure.

3. **RELATING:** The next best gift you can give your child is an authentic relationship with another person. If you're married, it's your spouse. You have two decades to present to your child how to live the Christ-life with fallen individuals. Think of your marriage like a TV reality show that your children get to watch every day—what a spectacular opportunity. Your kids will relate with fallen people all their lives, and you get to show them how to do it.

4. **REPENTING:** Failing is a daily occurrence. Failure is not the end of the world but the beginning of something unique. God has given you the world's greatest secret weapon: the power to change. Your mistakes are opportunities to transform, so you don't keep doing what you have done. The added benefit to personal transformation is you can teach your children how to change.

5. **LOVING:** Secure children are the by-product of loving parents. Insecure children are the by-product of fussy parents. Fussy parents will push their kids to find security in the culture. Their depravity will grow if you complicate their fallenness with yours. Your imitation of Christ will close the gap that separates your child from Christ.

6. **EXPORTING:** Christianity is an exportable religion. You are in the import/export business. Your response to what God is pouring into your life is to

pour it into your children. Living the gospel is not a passive exercise. Everything said thus far is what you should be pouring into your children: praying, being, relating, repenting, and loving.

7. **RELEASING:** Your job is not to save your kids; God does the saving. Your job is not to complicate what God can do. Be assured that God can regenerate any child despite the parents, but erecting hurdles doesn't have to happen. Instead, you want to cooperate with the Lord as you release your kids into the world as men and women who know how to submit to God while fulfilling the capacities and gifts that God has given to them.

Time to Parent

1. **PRAYING:** How do you know you trust the Lord to transform your children?

2. **BEING:** What elements of the fruit of the Spirit do you need to address?

3. **RELATING:** What does your marriage TV reality show reveal to your children?

4. **REPENTING:** Is your home an active repenting home? Please explain.

5. **LOVING:** How are you affecting your children with the love in your home?

6. **EXPORTING:** What needs to change to export Christ to your child?

7. **RELEASING:** As you look to your child's future release date, what do you need to change?

Day 29

One Reason Children Rebel

There is no fear in love, but perfect love casts out fear. For fear has to do with punishment, and whoever fears has not been perfected in love.

(1 John 4:18)

Parents are responsible and privileged to guide their children into a practical experience of knowing and loving God. Though all children are born with limited God-awareness, you can cooperate with the Lord in connecting that immature, innate awareness of God in practical ways that could lead to their salvation and progressive sanctification.

You primarily do this through your attitudes, words, and actions. These three characteristics become the most significant shaping influences that will motivate your kids to imitate or reject you, affecting how they respond to Jesus. Though you cannot make your children righteous or unrighteous, God calls you to cooperate with Him in their salvation. You do this by modeling the life of Christ before them (Ephesians 5:1) and teaching them all the things He taught you (Matthew 28:19-20).

If you are not modeling and teaching the life of Christ to your children, the chances of them rejecting your Christianity by the time they are teenagers are exponentially higher than if you humbly present Christ to them while they are young. The biggest culprit that hinders their thoughts about Christ is fear, which is one of the first sin patterns you'll see in their lives. So naturally, you want to be proactive in helping your child overcome fear. I've listed seven negative patterns for your consideration. If any of these represent you, it would be wise to remove them from your life.

- A distant parent
- An angry parent
- An abusive parent
- A critical parent
- A preoccupied parent
- An impatient parent
- A divorced parent

Some of these traits may be unavoidable, but you must know that they can become mental strongholds that will negatively shape your child (2 Corinthians 10:3-6). Being born in Adam is to be born with fear, which makes fearfulness part of everyone's Adamic wiring. Younger children are highly susceptible to fear; they need the security of a family community. If they do not find it, the temptation will be to hunt for a safer community outside their family when they age.

Running from fear and toward acceptance is one of the primary reasons a teen will distance himself from non-Christlike parents. He is looking for a more approving and loving community. Knowing this tendency and the accompanying temptations should motivate you to build a friendly and safe environment for your child. A simple biblical template to create this kind of home is the fruit of the Spirit constellation in Galatians 5:22-23. These nine elements give you a snapshot of what Christ was like and what you should be like to your children.

Examine Paul's template of Christlikeness to see how well you are doing and how you may need to change. You can preface each Christ trait with this question: "Are my children experiencing (the fruit of the Spirit) through me?"

- The love of Christ
- The joy of Christ
- The peace of Christ
- The patience of Christ
- The kindness of Christ
- The goodness of Christ
- The faithfulness of Christ
- The gentleness of Christ
- The self-control of Christ

You cannot save your children or make them holy, and you cannot live perfectly. But you can choose not to complicate their lives, which you can do if you give them the most precise picture of Jesus you can through your imprecise modeling.

Time to Parent

1. Talk to a friend, preferably your spouse, about how the fruit of the Spirit is manifesting in your life.
2. If there are areas that you need to change, detail a specific and practical plan to begin changing.

Day 30

Teach Them to Laugh at Themselves

A joyful heart is good medicine, but a crushed spirit dries up the bones.

(Proverbs 17:22)

If our children learn not to take themselves too seriously, it will be easier for them to live in relationships with others today and after they become adults. Not thinking too highly of yourself is to think humbly of yourself. A lack of gospel-centered humility keeps an individual from living well with God and others.

Have you ever gotten angry at someone? Anger is a lack of humility. Have you ever become impatient with someone? Impatience is a lack of humility. Humility is the foundational character trait of any individual's life. Without humility, there is no hope for any of us because God only gives empowering, life-changing favor to the humble (James 4:6). After Paul had finished the first three chapters of Ephesians, he transitioned his message to practically living out the gospel. Ephesians is divided neatly into two parts. Many years ago, an old preacher told me, "Brother Thomas, the Book of Ephesians is in two parts. Part one teaches you how to be saved. Part two teaches you how to behave." He is correct. Paul teaches profound theology in the first part and how to live it out in the second. And where does he begin part two? It's humility: thinking less of yourself and more of others (Ephesians 4:1-2).

Thinking less of ourselves is one reason we laugh a lot in our home. The humble person will laugh a lot. He will especially laugh at himself. The over-sensitive, approval-driven person is not free to do this, especially to himself. He is too busy thinking too highly of himself while demanding that others also think highly of him. The thought of anyone thinking less of him, even with appropriate humor, is unbearable. It's this kind of over-sensitivity and insecurity that kills relationships. Humor is one way to practice humility.

> Laughter is a divine gift to the human who is humble. A proud man cannot laugh because he must watch his dignity; he cannot give himself over to the rocking and rolling of his belly. But a poor and happy man laughs heartily because he gives no serious attention to his ego.... Only the truly humble belong to this kingdom of divine laughter... Humor and humility should keep good company. Self-deprecating humor can be a healthy reminder that we are not the center of the universe, that humility is our proper posture before our fellow humans as well as before Almighty God...[1]

Laughter is not the only response to pride, but it's an effective one. Too many people are too serious, too angry, too hurt, and too demanding. They don't laugh anymore unless they are laughing at others. The gospel-centered person is free to laugh at himself because he has nothing to protect, nothing to hide, and nothing to demand. He is

1 Terry Lindvall (*Surprised by Laughter: The Comic World of C. S. Lewis*)

soberly aware that the Son of God died on the cross so he can be set free from the power and bondage of sin. "If the Son sets you free, you will be free indeed" (John 8:36). The humble person is reminded daily of the gospel and quickly lives in the good of it. He is free to laugh a lot, especially at himself.

Time to Parent

Heaven is a place of unbridled laughter, joy, praise, and worship. The gospel-freed person can begin practicing a little heaven on earth today.

1. Do you laugh a lot? Are you free to laugh at yourself? If not, why not?
2. How do you characterize yourself? More sensitive than secure? More touchy than tender? More frustrated than free? Please explain.
3. How does your attitude about life and others affect your child? How do you need to change?

Day 31

You Cannot Change Children

I planted, Apollos watered, but God gave the growth.
(1 Corinthians 3:6)

One of the hardest things a Christian parent will ever experience is a child choosing not to walk with the Lord. The temptation to force or manipulate righteousness on the child is attached to this personal struggle. You'll know if you're susceptible to these struggles if you are over-worrying, over-caring, or over-trying to get your child to change.

Typically, these temptations only happen with those who are closest to us—spouses and children. Thus, we are freer from the lostness of and less tempted to worry about those who are not within our immediate relational spheres. Jesus had the remarkable ability to care well for everyone regardless of His biological relationship with them. He wept for the stubborn people in Jerusalem (Matthew 23:37). He unemotionally explained how being related to Him did not give His family special privileges (Matthew 12:48). The biblio-centric sweet spot is not to over-care or under care for those who need the Lord. You will find that rest after you learn that you cannot change anyone, including your children. Anxiety or anger will not bring people into the Kingdom of God: The anxious parent does not trust the

Lord; the angry parent does not trust the Lord. Both of these parental demographics have forgotten how cooperating with the Lord in the spiritual maturity of their children has a stopping point.

Paul identified that stopping point right after planting and watering, just before God gives the growth. So perhaps it would be helpful if you put a period after the word "watered" in 1 Corinthians 3:6 as a reminder that personal responsibility for the redemption of others stops there as you wait for the Lord to provide the necessary change in a person's life. Then, you will quickly know if you've blown through the sweet spot if you try to manipulate your child to trust Christ. Fear and anger are two manipulative strategies for parents of rebellious children, and regret and self-condemnation typically accompany fear and anger. These parents are not trusting the Lord. Grace is the means God uses to save individuals, not your works (Ephesians 2:8-9). If your child turns to the Lord, it will be because of God's empowering favor, which is something you can't manipulate. If your child is not walking with Jesus and you are struggling with anxiety, anger, regret, or self-condemnation, you must reexamine how you relate to God.

In this 31-day devotional, I have consistently called you to assess your life, marriage, and children as you cooperate with the Lord to make the necessary changes in you so you can help your kids love God and others. I have asked you to water and plant only. I have not requested or expected you to provide the growth they need to live for God. There is active and passive obedience. Active obedience is what you're supposed to do. Passive obedience is what God does to you. You must functionally know the difference, which you'll perceive through the grid of anger, regret, anxiousness, or self-condemnation.

If you are struggling in any of these areas, the Lord may be using your wayward child as a means to parent you into biblical faith. The irony is that if you struggle unnecessarily over your kid's waywardness, you're doing something similar to what your child is doing: not trusting God. So, the first step in parenting your child is to parent yourself.

Time to Parent

1. What hinders you from fully trusting God to change your child?
2. Write out the sin pattern(s) that hinder you and make a plan to change while you trust God to change your kid.

About the Author

 Rick Thomas launched the Life Over Coffee global training network in 2008 to bring hope and help for you and others by creating resources that spark conversations for transformation. His primary responsibilities are resource creation and leadership development, which he does through speaking, writing, podcasting, and educating. In 1990 he earned a BA in Theology and, in 1991, a BS in Education. In 1993, he received his ordination into Christian ministry, and in 2000, he graduated with an MA in Counseling from The Master's University. In 2006, he was recognized as a Fellow of the Association of Certified Biblical Counselors (ACBC).

Other Books Available from
Life Over Coffee

Boasting in Weakness
Centering Your Marriage on Christ
Communication
Complete Marriage
Don't Apologize
Exchange the Truth for a Lie
Help My Marriage Has Grown Cold
Identity Crisis
Local Church
Loving Me
Mad
Marriage Devotion We Are One
Politics and Culture
Parenting Devotion from Zero to Adulthood
Sex, Temptation, and Modesty
Storm Hurler
The Cyber Effect
The Talk
Wives Leading
You Decide